This book belongs to an awesome Soccer Player called:

camille

Year: **2021**

Remember, everything you need to be great is already inside you

About Me

Birthday _____ Age ____ Grade ____

School _____

I play soccer with _____

Favorite position: _____

Best position: _____

Favorite skill: _____

Strengths:

Hard Worker ☐   Speed ☐   Stamina ☐   Shooting ☐

Dribbling ☐   Defending ☐   Attitude ☐   Receiving ☐

Other ☐   _____

Started socccer (when) _____

Best soccer game so far :

_____

_____

Notes _____

_____

_____

I love playing soccer because....

_____

_____

_____

Favorite soccer players _____

_____

Favorite soccer coach _____

Design your own soccer kit

Colors _____

_____

Notes _____

_____

_____

Other items

_____

My Team Mates

Most Skillful _____

Funniest _____

Chattiest _____

Bravest _____

Training Schedule

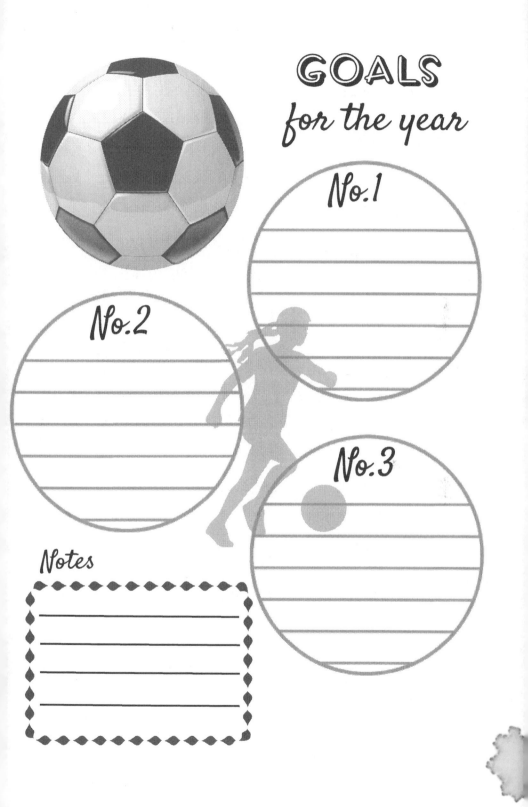

GOALS
for the year

No.1

No.2

No.3

Notes

December
Week 1

Monday

Tuesday

Wednesday

Thursday

Friday

Saturday

Sunday

Priorities

To Do

★

★

★

★

★

Game Details

Match Review

Date _____ / _____ / _____

Opponent _____

Game played 🏠   🚗

Positions Played

Goalie ☐   Defense ☐

Midfield ☐   Forward ☐

Goals Scored ⚽ ⚽ ⚽ ⚽ ⚽ ⚽

Highlights

_____

_____

Coach Said

_____

_____

Final Score: _____ W / L

How I felt

January
Week 2

Monday

Tuesday

Wednesday

Thursday

Friday

Saturday

Sunday

Priorities

★

★

★

★

★

Match Review

Date _____ / _____ / _____

Opponent _____

Game played 🏠   🚗

Positions Played
Goalie ☐   Defense ☐
Midfield ☐   Forward ☐

Goals Scored ⚽ ⚽ ⚽ ⚽ ⚽ ⚽

Highlights

_____

_____

Coach Said

_____

_____

Final Score: _____ W / L

How I felt

January
Week 3

Monday

Tuesday

Wednesday

Thursday

Friday

Saturday

Sunday

Priorities

- ★
- ★
- ★
- ★
- ★

Match Review

Date _____ / _____ / _____

Opponent _____

Game played 🏠   🚗

Positions Played

Goalie ☐   Defense ☐

Midfield ☐   Forward ☐

Goals Scored ⚽ ⚽ ⚽ ⚽ ⚽ ⚽

Highlights

_____

_____

Coach Said

_____

_____

Final Score: W / L

How I felt   ☹️   🙁   😐   🙂   😃

January
Week 4

DREAM IT. WISH IT. DO IT.

Monday	**Priorities**
Tuesday	
Wednesday	
Thursday	★
	★
	★
Friday	★
	★
Saturday	
Sunday	

Match Review

Date _____ / _____ / _____

Opponent _____

Game played 🏠 🚗

Positions Played
Goalie ☐   Defense ☐

Midfield ☐   Forward ☐

Goals Scored ⚽ ⚽ ⚽ ⚽ ⚽ ⚽

Highlights

_____

_____

Coach Said

_____

_____

Final Score: W / L

How I felt 😞 🙁 😐 🙂 😃

January
Week 5

Monday

Tuesday

Wednesday

Thursday

Friday

Saturday

Sunday

Priorities

★

★

★

★

★

Match Review

Date _____ / _____ / _____

Opponent _____

Game played 🏠 🚗

Positions Played
Goalie ☐ Defense ☐
Midfield ☐ Forward ☐

Goals Scored ⚽ ⚽ ⚽ ⚽ ⚽ ⚽

Highlights

_____
_____

Coach Said

_____
_____

Final Score: _____ W / L

How I felt

February

Week 6

Monday

Tuesday

Wednesday

Thursday

Friday

Saturday

Sunday

Priorities

★

★

★

★

★

Match Review

Date _____ / _____ / _____

Opponent _____

Game played 🏠   🚗

Positions Played

Goalie ☐   Defense ☐

Midfield ☐   Forward ☐

Goals Scored ⚽ ⚽ ⚽ ⚽ ⚽ ⚽

Highlights

_____

_____

Coach Said

_____

_____

Final Score: W / L

How I felt

February

Week 7

Monday

Tuesday

Wednesday

Thursday

Friday

Saturday

Sunday

Priorities

- ★
- ★
- ★
- ★
- ★

Match Review

Date _____ / _____ / _____

Opponent _____

Game played 🏠   🚗

Positions Played

Goalie ☐   Defense ☐

Midfield ☐   Forward ☐

Goals Scored ⚽ ⚽ ⚽ ⚽ ⚽ ⚽

Highlights

_____

_____

Coach Said

_____

_____

Final Score: _____ W / L

How I felt

February
Week 8

WAKE UP WITH DETERMINATION.
GO TO BED WITH SATISFACTION.

Monday

Tuesday

Wednesday

Thursday

Friday

Saturday

Sunday

Priorities

★
★
★
★
★

Match Review

Date _____ / _____ / _____

Opponent _____

Game played 🏠 🚗

Positions Played   Goalie ☐   Defense ☐

   Midfield ☐   Forward ☐

Goals Scored ⚽ ⚽ ⚽ ⚽ ⚽ ⚽

Highlights

_____

_____

Coach Said

_____

_____

Final Score: W / L

How I felt   ☹ 🙁 😐 🙂 😃

February
Week 9

Monday

Tuesday

Wednesday

Thursday

Friday

Saturday

Sunday

Priorities

★

★

★

★

★

Match Review

Date _____ / _____ / _____

Opponent _____

Game played 🏠   🚚

Positions Played   Goalie ☐   Defense ☐
                    Midfield ☐   Forward ☐

Goals Scored ⚽ ⚽ ⚽ ⚽ ⚽ ⚽

Highlights

_____

_____

Coach Said

_____

_____

Final Score: _____ W / L

How I felt

March
Week 10

LITTLE THINGS MAKE BIG DAYS.

Monday

Tuesday

Wednesday

Thursday

Friday

Saturday

Sunday

Priorities

- ★
- ★
- ★
- ★
- ★

Match Review

Date _____ / _____ / _____

Opponent _____

Game played 🏠 🚗

Positions Played
Goalie ☐   Defense ☐
Midfield ☐   Forward ☐

Goals Scored ⚽ ⚽ ⚽ ⚽ ⚽ ⚽

Highlights

_____

_____

Coach Said

_____

_____

Final Score: _____ W / L

How I felt

March
Week 11

Priorities

Monday

Tuesday

Wednesday

Thursday

Friday

Saturday

Sunday

★

★

★

★

★

Match Review

Date _____ / _____ / _____

Opponent _____

Game played 🏠   🚗

Positions Played

Goalie ☐   Defense ☐

Midfield ☐   Forward ☐

Goals Scored ⚽ ⚽ ⚽ ⚽ ⚽ ⚽

Highlights

_____

_____

Coach Said

_____

_____

Final Score: W / L

How I felt

March
Week 12

Monday

Tuesday

Wednesday

Thursday

Friday

Saturday

Sunday

Priorities

★

★

★

★

★

Match Review

Date _____ / _____ / _____

Opponent _____

Game played 🏠   🚗

Positions Played

Goalie ☐   Defense ☐

Midfield ☐   Forward ☐

Goals Scored ⚽ ⚽ ⚽ ⚽ ⚽ ⚽

Highlights

_____

_____

Coach Said

_____

_____

Final Score: _____ W / L

How I felt

March
Week 13

Monday

Tuesday

Wednesday

Thursday

Friday

Saturday

Sunday

Priorities

★

★

★

★

★

Match Review

Date _____ / _____ / _____

Opponent _____

Game played 🏠　　🚗

Positions Played
Goalie ☐　　Defense ☐
Midfield ☐　　Forward ☐

Goals Scored ⚽ ⚽ ⚽ ⚽ ⚽ ⚽

Highlights

_____

_____

Coach Said

_____

_____

Final Score: 　　　　　　　W / L

How I felt 🙁 😕 😐 🙂 😃

April
Week 14

Monday

Tuesday

Wednesday

Thursday

Friday

Saturday

Sunday

Priorities

★
★
★
★
★

Match Review

Date _____ / _____ / _____

Opponent _____

Game played 🏠   🚚

Positions Played

Goalie ☐   Defense ☐

Midfield ☐   Forward ☐

Goals Scored ⚽ ⚽ ⚽ ⚽ ⚽ ⚽

Highlights

_____

_____

Coach Said

_____

_____

Final Score: W / L

How I felt   ☹   😐   😐   🙂   😃

April
Week 15

Monday

Tuesday

Wednesday

Thursday

Friday

Saturday

Sunday

Priorities

★

★

★

★

★

Match Review

Date _____ / _____ / _____

Opponent _____

Game played 🏠 🚚

Positions Played

Goalie ☐   Defense ☐

Midfield ☐   Forward ☐

Goals Scored ⚽ ⚽ ⚽ ⚽ ⚽ ⚽

Highlights

_____

_____

Coach Said

_____

_____

Final Score: _____ W / L

How I felt

April
Week 16

Monday

Tuesday

Wednesday

Thursday

Friday

Saturday

Sunday

Priorities

★

★

★

★

★

Match Review

Date _____ / _____ / _____

Opponent _____

Game played 🏠 🚗

Positions Played

Goalie ☐ Defense ☐

Midfield ☐ Forward ☐

Goals Scored ⚽ ⚽ ⚽ ⚽ ⚽ ⚽

Highlights

_____

_____

Coach Said

_____

_____

Final Score: W / L

How I felt

April
Week 17

Monday

Tuesday

Wednesday

Thursday

Friday

Saturday

Sunday

Priorities

★

★

★

★

★

Match Review

Date _____ / _____ / _____

Opponent _____

Game played 🏠 🚗

Positions Played   Goalie ☐   Defense ☐

Midfield ☐   Forward ☐

Goals Scored ⚽ ⚽ ⚽ ⚽ ⚽ ⚽

Highlights

_____

_____

Coach Said

_____

_____

Final Score: _____ W / L

How I felt   ☹ 😕 😐 🙂 😃

April
Week 18

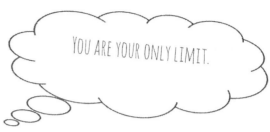

YOU ARE YOUR ONLY LIMIT.

Monday

Tuesday

Wednesday

Thursday

Friday

Saturday

Sunday

Priorities

★

★

★

★

★

Match Review

Date _____ / _____ / _____

Opponent _____

Game played 🏠   🚗

Positions Played Goalie ☐   Defense ☐
Midfield ☐   Forward ☐

Goals Scored ⚽ ⚽ ⚽ ⚽ ⚽ ⚽

Highlights

_____

_____

Coach Said

_____

_____

Final Score: _____ W / L

How I felt

May
Week 19

Monday

Tuesday

Wednesday

Thursday

Friday

Saturday

Sunday

Priorities

★

★

★

★

★

Match Review

Date _____ / _____ / _____

Opponent _____

Game played 🏠 🚗

Positions Played

Goalie ☐   Defense ☐

Midfield ☐   Forward ☐

Goals Scored ⚽ ⚽ ⚽ ⚽ ⚽ ⚽

Highlights

_____

_____

Coach Said

_____

_____

Final Score: W / L

How I felt   ☹   🙁   😐   🙂   😄

May
Week 20

I CAN AND I WILL.

Monday

Tuesday

Wednesday

Thursday

Friday

Saturday

Sunday

Priorities

★

★

★

★

★

Match Review

Date _____ / _____ / _____

Opponent _____

Game played 🏠 🚗

Positions Played

Goalie ☐ Defense ☐

Midfield ☐ Forward ☐

Goals Scored ⚽ ⚽ ⚽ ⚽ ⚽ ⚽

Highlights

_____

_____

Coach Said

_____

_____

Final Score: _____ W / L

How I felt ☹ 😕 😐 🙂 😄

May
Week 21

IT NEVER GETS EASIER -
YOU JUST GET BETTER.

Monday

Tuesday

Wednesday

Thursday

Friday

Saturday

Sunday

Priorities

★

★

★

★

★

Match Review

Date _____ / _____ / _____

Opponent _____

Game played 🏠 🚗

Positions Played

Goalie ☐   Defense ☐

Midfield ☐   Forward ☐

Goals Scored ⚽ ⚽ ⚽ ⚽ ⚽ ⚽

Highlights

_____

_____

Coach Said

_____

_____

Final Score: _____ W / L

How I felt 🙁 😕 😐 🙂 😄

May
Week 22

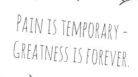

PAIN IS TEMPORARY -
GREATNESS IS FOREVER.

Monday

Tuesday

Wednesday

Thursday

Friday

Saturday

Sunday

Priorities

★

★

★

★

★

Match Review

Date _____ / _____ / _____

Opponent _____

Game played 🏠   🚗

Positions Played

Goalie ☐   Defense ☐

Midfield ☐   Forward ☐

Goals Scored ⚽ ⚽ ⚽ ⚽ ⚽ ⚽

Highlights

_____

_____

Coach Said

_____

_____

Final Score: _____ W / L

How I felt ☹ 🙁 😐 🙂 😃

June
Week 23

YOU ARE STRONGER THAN YOU THINK.

Monday

Tuesday

Wednesday

Thursday

Friday

Saturday

Sunday

Priorities

★

★

★

★

★

Match Review

Date _____ / _____ / _____

Opponent _____

Game played 🏠 🚗

Positions Played

Goalie ☐   Defense ☐

Midfield ☐   Forward ☐

Goals Scored ⚽ ⚽ ⚽ ⚽ ⚽ ⚽

Highlights

_____

_____

Coach Said

_____

_____

Final Score: _____ W / L

How I felt

June
Week 24

Monday

Tuesday

Wednesday

Thursday

Friday

Saturday

Sunday

Priorities

★
★
★
★
★

Match Review

Date _____ / _____ / _____

Opponent _____

Game played 🏠   🚗

Positions Played

Goalie ☐   Defense ☐

Midfield ☐   Forward ☐

Goals Scored ⚽ ⚽ ⚽ ⚽ ⚽ ⚽

Highlights

_____

_____

Coach Said

_____

_____

Final Score: W / L

How I felt ☹ 🙁 😐 🙂 😃

June
Week 25

Monday

Tuesday

Wednesday

Thursday

Friday

Saturday

Sunday

Priorities

★
★
★
★
★

Match Review

Date _____/_____/_____

Opponent _____

Game played 🏠 🚙

Positions Played

Goalie ☐ Defense ☐

Midfield ☐ Forward ☐

Goals Scored ⚽ ⚽ ⚽ ⚽ ⚽ ⚽

Highlights

_____

_____

Coach Said

_____

_____

Final Score: _____ W / L

How I felt

June

Week 26

Monday

Tuesday

Wednesday

Thursday

Friday

Saturday

Sunday

Priorities

★

★

★

★

★

Match Review

Date _____ / _____ / _____

Opponent _____

Game played 🏠 🚗

Positions Played

Goalie ☐ Defense ☐

Midfield ☐ Forward ☐

Goals Scored ⚽ ⚽ ⚽ ⚽ ⚽ ⚽

Highlights

_____

_____

Coach Said

_____

_____

Final Score: W / L

How I felt ☹ 😕 😐 🙂 😃

July
Week 27

Monday

Tuesday

Wednesday

Thursday

Friday

Saturday

Sunday

Priorities

★

★

★

★

★

Match Review

Date _____ / _____ / _____

Opponent _____

Game played 🏠 🚗

Positions Played

Goalie ☐   Defense ☐

Midfield ☐   Forward ☐

Goals Scored ⚽ ⚽ ⚽ ⚽ ⚽ ⚽

Highlights

_____

_____

Coach Said

_____

_____

Final Score: _____ W / L

How I felt

July
Week 28

TAKE YOUR DREAMS SERIOUSLY.

Monday

Tuesday

Wednesday

Thursday

Friday

Saturday

Sunday

Priorities

★
★
★
★
★

Match Review

Date _____ / _____ / _____

Opponent _____

Game played 🏠 🚗

Positions Played

Goalie ☐   Defense ☐

Midfield ☐   Forward ☐

Goals Scored ⚽ ⚽ ⚽ ⚽ ⚽ ⚽

Highlights

_____

_____

Coach Said

_____

_____

Final Score: W / L

How I felt 🙁 🙂 😐 🙂 😀

July
Week 29

Monday

Tuesday

Wednesday

Thursday

Friday

Saturday

Sunday

Priorities

- ★
- ★
- ★
- ★
- ★

Match Review

Date _____/_____/_____

Opponent _____

Game played 🏠 🚗

Positions Played

Goalie ☐   Defense ☐

Midfield ☐   Forward ☐

Goals Scored ⚽ ⚽ ⚽ ⚽ ⚽ ⚽

Highlights

_____

_____

Coach Said

_____

_____

Final Score: W / L

How I felt

July
Week 30

WORK HARD - DREAM BIG.

Monday

Tuesday

Wednesday

Thursday

Friday

Saturday

Sunday

Priorities

- ★
- ★
- ★
- ★
- ★

Match Review

Date _____/_____/_____

Opponent _____

Game played 🏠 🚗

Positions Played

Goalie ☐   Defense ☐

Midfield ☐   Forward ☐

Goals Scored ⚽ ⚽ ⚽ ⚽ ⚽ ⚽

Highlights

_____

_____

Coach Said

_____

_____

Final Score: W / L

How I felt

July
Week 31

Monday

Tuesday

Wednesday

Thursday

Friday

Saturday

Sunday

Priorities

★

★

★

★

★

Match Review

Date _____ / _____ / _____

Opponent _____

Game played 🏠 🚙

Positions Played

Goalie ☐   Defense ☐

Midfield ☐   Forward ☐

Goals Scored ⚽ ⚽ ⚽ ⚽ ⚽ ⚽

Highlights

_____

_____

Coach Said

_____

_____

Final Score: W / L

How I felt 🙁 🙂 😐 🙂 😄

August
Week 32

Monday

Tuesday

Wednesday

Thursday

Friday

Saturday

Sunday

Priorities

★

★

★

★

★

Match Review

Date _____ / _____ / _____

Opponent _____

Game played 🏠 🚗

Positions Played

Goalie ☐   Defense ☐

Midfield ☐   Forward ☐

Goals Scored ⚽ ⚽ ⚽ ⚽ ⚽ ⚽

Highlights

_____

_____

Coach Said

_____

_____

Final Score: W / L

How I felt   ☹ 😕 😐 🙂 😀

August
Week 33

Monday

Tuesday

Wednesday

Thursday

Friday

Saturday

Sunday

Priorities

★

★

★

★

★

Match Review

Date _____ / _____ / _____

Opponent _____

Game played 🏠 🚗

Positions Played

Goalie ☐   Defense ☐

Midfield ☐   Forward ☐

Goals Scored ⚽ ⚽ ⚽ ⚽ ⚽ ⚽

Highlights

_____

_____

Coach Said

_____

_____

Final Score: _____ W / L

How I felt 😞 😕 😐 🙂 😄

August
Week 34

BE DRIVEN.

Monday	
Tuesday	
Wednesday	
Thursday	
Friday	
Saturday	
Sunday	

Priorities

★

★

★

★

★

Match Review

Date _____ / _____ / _____

Opponent _____

Game played 🏠   🚗

Positions Played

Goalie ☐   Defense ☐

Midfield ☐   Forward ☐

Goals Scored ⚽ ⚽ ⚽ ⚽ ⚽ ⚽

Highlights

_____

_____

Coach Said

_____

_____

Final Score: _____   W / L

How I felt ☹ 🙁 😐 🙂 😃

August
Week 35

Monday

Tuesday

Wednesday

Thursday

Friday

Saturday

Sunday

Priorities

- ★
- ★
- ★
- ★
- ★

Match Review

Date _____ / _____ / _____

Opponent _____

Game played 🏠 🚗

Positions Played
Goalie ☐ Defense ☐
Midfield ☐ Forward ☐

Goals Scored ⚽ ⚽ ⚽ ⚽ ⚽ ⚽

Highlights

_____

_____

Coach Said

_____

_____

Final Score: _____ W / L

How I felt ☹ 😐 😐 🙂 😀

September
Week 36

BE POSITIVE.

Monday

Tuesday

Wednesday

Thursday

Friday

Saturday

Sunday

Priorities

★
★
★
★
★

Match Review

Date _____ / _____ / _____

Opponent _____

Game played 🏠 🚗

Positions Played

Goalie ☐ Defense ☐

Midfield ☐ Forward ☐

Goals Scored ⚽ ⚽ ⚽ ⚽ ⚽ ⚽

Highlights

_____

_____

Coach Said

_____

_____

Final Score: _____ W / L

How I felt ☹ 🙁 😐 🙂 😄

September
Week 37

Monday

Tuesday

Wednesday

Thursday

Friday

Saturday

Sunday

Priorities

★
★
★
★
★

Match Review

Date _____ / _____ / _____

Opponent _____

Game played 🏠 🚗

Positions Played
Goalie ☐   Defense ☐
Midfield ☐   Forward ☐

Goals Scored ⚽ ⚽ ⚽ ⚽ ⚽ ⚽

Highlights

_____

_____

Coach Said

_____

_____

Final Score: _____ W / L

How I felt   ☹ 🙁 😐 🙂 😀

September
Week 38

Monday

Tuesday

Wednesday

Thursday

Friday

Saturday

Sunday

Priorities

★

★

★

★

★

Match Review

Date _____ / _____ / _____

Opponent _____

Game played 🏠 🚗

Positions Played
Goalie ☐   Defense ☐
Midfield ☐   Forward ☐

Goals Scored ⚽ ⚽ ⚽ ⚽ ⚽ ⚽

Highlights

_____

_____

Coach Said

_____

_____

Final Score: _____ W / L

How I felt ☹ 🙁 😐 🙂 😃

September
Week 39

Monday

Tuesday

Wednesday

Thursday

Friday

Saturday

Sunday

Priorities

★

★

★

★

★

Match Review

Date _____/_____/_____

Opponent _____

Game played 🏠 🚗

Positions Played

Goalie ☐   Defense ☐

Midfield ☐   Forward ☐

Goals Scored ⚽ ⚽ ⚽ ⚽ ⚽ ⚽

Highlights

_____

_____

Coach Said

_____

_____

Final Score: W / L

How I felt   ☹ 😕 😐 🙂 😃

September
Week 40

Monday

Tuesday

Wednesday

Thursday

Friday

Saturday

Sunday

Priorities

- ★
- ★
- ★
- ★
- ★

Match Review

Date _____ / _____ / _____

Opponent _____

Game played 🏠   🚗

Positions Played

Goalie ☐   Defense ☐

Midfield ☐   Forward ☐

Goals Scored ⚽ ⚽ ⚽ ⚽ ⚽ ⚽

Highlights

_____

_____

Coach Said

_____

_____

Final Score: W / L

How I felt   ☹️ 🙁 😐 🙂 😄

October

Week 41

Monday

Tuesday

Wednesday

Thursday

Friday

Saturday

Sunday

Priorities

★

★

★

★

★

Match Review

Date _____/_____/_____

Opponent _____

Game played 🏠   🚗

Positions Played

Goalie ☐   Defense ☐

Midfield ☐   Forward ☐

Goals Scored ⚽ ⚽ ⚽ ⚽ ⚽ ⚽

Highlights

_____

_____

Coach Said

_____

_____

Final Score: W / L

How I felt ☹ 😐 😐 🙂 😀

October

Week 42

Monday

Tuesday

Wednesday

Thursday

Friday

Saturday

Sunday

Priorities

★

★

★

★

★

Match Review

Date _____ / _____ / _____

Opponent _____

Game played 🏠   🚗

Positions Played

Goalie ☐   Defense ☐

Midfield ☐   Forward ☐

Goals Scored ⚽ ⚽ ⚽ ⚽ ⚽ ⚽

Highlights

_____

_____

Coach Said

_____

_____

Final Score: W / L

How I felt   ☹   🙁   😐   🙂   😃

October
Week 43

Priorities

Monday

Tuesday

Wednesday

Thursday

Friday

Saturday

Sunday

- ★
- ★
- ★
- ★
- ★

Match Review

Date _____ / _____ / _____

Opponent _____

Game played 🏠　　🚗

Positions Played

Goalie ☐　　Defense ☐

Midfield ☐　　Forward ☐

Goals Scored ⚽ ⚽ ⚽ ⚽ ⚽ ⚽

Highlights

_____

_____

Coach Said

_____

_____

Final Score: _____ W / L

How I felt ☹ 🙁 😐 🙂 😄

October

Week 44

Monday

Tuesday

Wednesday

Thursday

Friday

Saturday

Sunday

Priorities

★

★

★

★

★

Match Review

Date _____ / _____ / _____

Opponent _____

Game played 🏠 🚗

Positions Played

Goalie ☐   Defense ☐

Midfield ☐   Forward ☐

Goals Scored ⚽ ⚽ ⚽ ⚽ ⚽ ⚽

Highlights

_____

_____

Coach Said

_____

_____

Final Score: W / L

How I felt   ☹ 🙁 😐 🙂 😃

November

Week 45

Monday

Tuesday

Wednesday

Thursday

Friday

Saturday

Sunday

Priorities

★

★

★

★

★

Match Review

Date _____ / _____ / _____

Opponent _____

Game played 🏠 🚗

Positions Played

Goalie ☐ Defense ☐

Midfield ☐ Forward ☐

Goals Scored ⚽ ⚽ ⚽ ⚽ ⚽ ⚽

Highlights

_____

_____

Coach Said

_____

_____

Final Score: _____ W / L

How I felt ☹ 😐 😐 🙂 😄

November
Week 46

Monday

Tuesday

Wednesday

Thursday

Friday

Saturday

Sunday

Priorities

★

★

★

★

★

Match Review

Date _____/_____/_____

Opponent _____

Game played 🏠 🚚

Positions Played
Goalie ☐   Defense ☐
Midfield ☐   Forward ☐

Goals Scored ⚽ ⚽ ⚽ ⚽ ⚽ ⚽

Highlights

_____

_____

Coach Said

_____

_____

Final Score: W / L

How I felt ☹ 🙁 😐 🙂 😃

November

Week 47

Monday

Tuesday

Wednesday

Thursday

Friday

Saturday

Sunday

Priorities

To Do

- ★
- ★
- ★
- ★
- ★

Game Details

Match Review

Date _____ / _____ / _____

Opponent _____

Game played 🏠 🚗

Positions Played   Goalie ☐   Defense ☐

Midfield ☐   Forward ☐

Goals Scored ⚽ ⚽ ⚽ ⚽ ⚽ ⚽

Highlights

_____

_____

Coach Said

_____

_____

Final Score: W / L

How I felt   ☹ 🙁 😐 🙂 😃

November

Week 48

BE A LIGHT TO THE WORLD.

Monday

Tuesday

Wednesday

Thursday

Friday

Saturday

Sunday

Priorities

★

★

★

★

★

Match Review

Date _____ / _____ / _____

Opponent _____

Game played 🏠   🚗

Positions Played   Goalie ☐   Defense ☐

              Midfield ☐   Forward ☐

Goals Scored ⚽ ⚽ ⚽ ⚽ ⚽ ⚽

Highlights

_____

_____

Coach Said

_____

_____

Final Score: W / L

How I felt ☹ 😕 😐 🙂 😄

December
Week 49

Monday

Tuesday

Wednesday

Thursday

Friday

Saturday

Sunday

Priorities

★
★
★
★
★

Match Review

Date _____ / _____ / _____

Opponent _____

Game played 🏠 🚗

Positions Played

Goalie ☐   Defense ☐

Midfield ☐   Forward ☐

Goals Scored ⚽ ⚽ ⚽ ⚽ ⚽ ⚽

Highlights

_____

_____

Coach Said

_____

_____

Final Score: _____ W / L

How I felt ☹ 😕 😐 🙂 😃

December

Week 50

Monday

Tuesday

Wednesday

Thursday

Friday

Saturday

Sunday

Priorities

★

★

★

★

★

Match Review

Date _____ / _____ / _____

Opponent _____

Game played 🏠 🚗

Positions Played   Goalie ☐   Defense ☐

Midfield ☐   Forward ☐

Goals Scored ⚽ ⚽ ⚽ ⚽ ⚽ ⚽

Highlights

_____

_____

Coach Said

_____

_____

Final Score: _____   W / L

How I felt   ☹ 😕 😐 🙂 😀

December

Week 51

Monday

Tuesday

Wednesday

Thursday

Friday

Saturday

Sunday

Priorities

★

★

★

★

★

Match Review

Date _____ / _____ / _____

Opponent _____

Game played 🏠　　🚗

Positions Played
Goalie ☐　　Defense ☐
Midfield ☐　　Forward ☐

Goals Scored ⚽ ⚽ ⚽ ⚽ ⚽ ⚽

Highlights

_____

_____

Coach Said

_____

_____

Final Score: _____ W / L

How I felt ☹ 🙁 😐 🙂 😃

December

Week 52

Monday

Tuesday

Wednesday

Thursday

Friday

Saturday

Sunday

Priorities

★

★

★

★

★

Match Review

Date _____ / _____ / _____

Opponent _____

Game played 🏠   🚗

Positions Played
Goalie ☐   Defense ☐
Midfield ☐   Forward ☐

Goals Scored ⚽ ⚽ ⚽ ⚽ ⚽ ⚽

Highlights

_____

_____

Coach Said

_____

_____

Final Score: _____ W / L

How I felt ☹️ 🙂 😐 🙂 😄

Tactics and Strategy Ideas

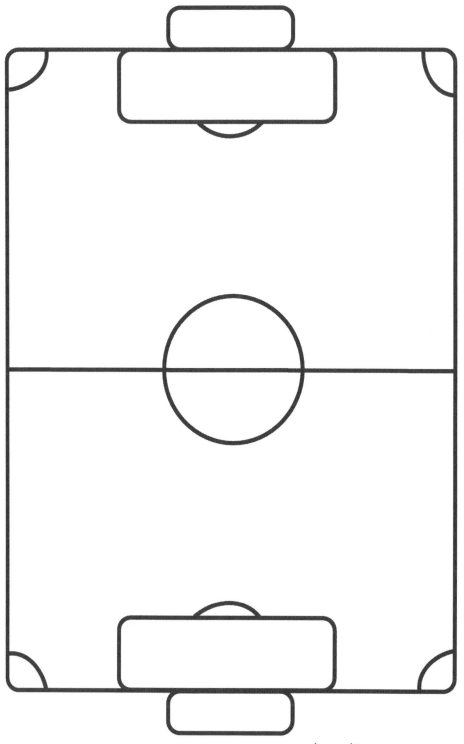

or even some soccer doodles

Tactics and Strategy Ideas

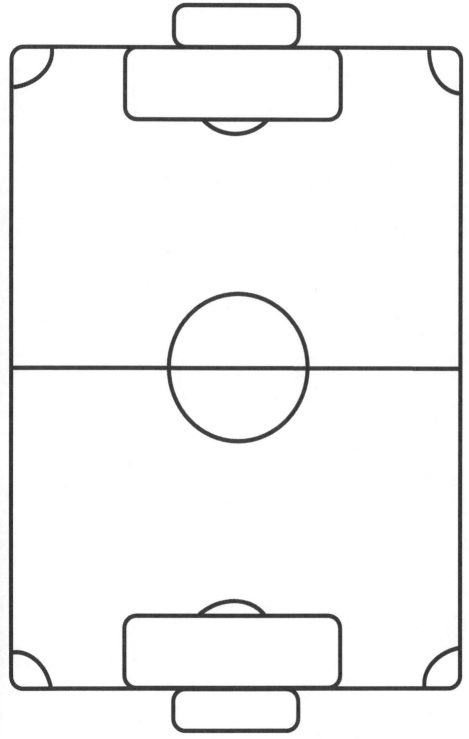

or even some soccer doodles

Tactics and Strategy Ideas

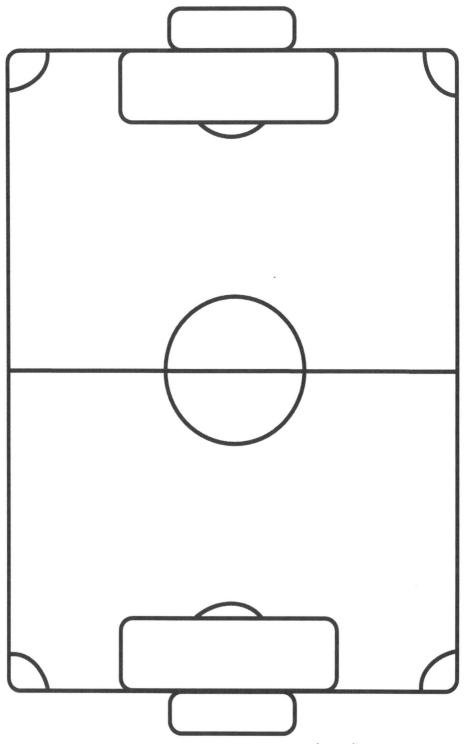

or even some soccer doodles

Tactics and Strategy Ideas

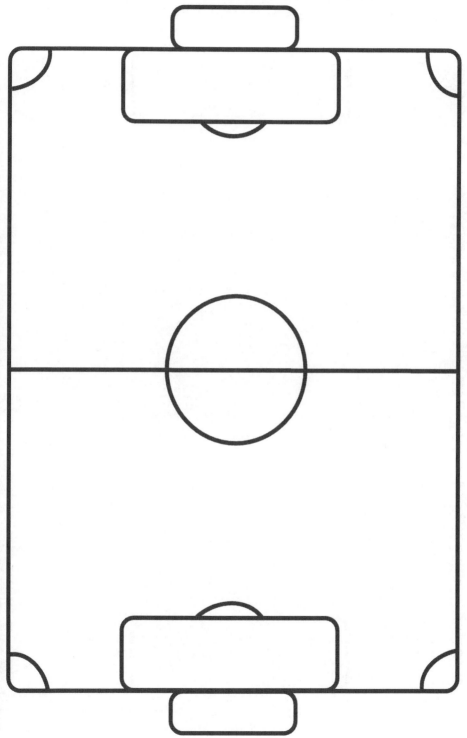

or even some soccer doodles

Tactics and Strategy Ideas

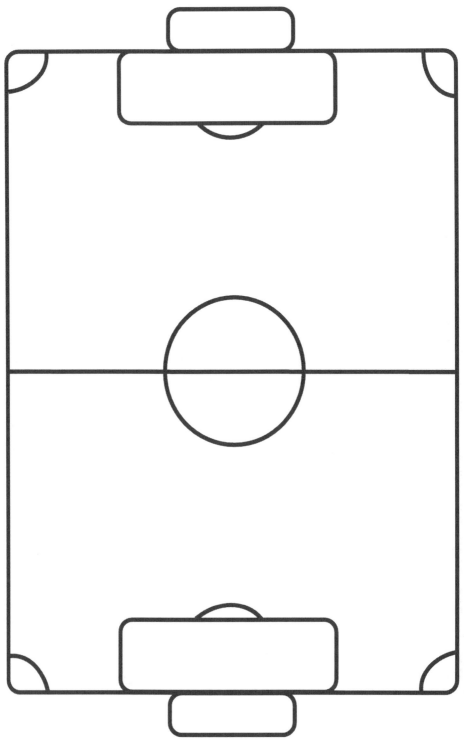

or even some soccer doodles

Tactics and Strategy Ideas

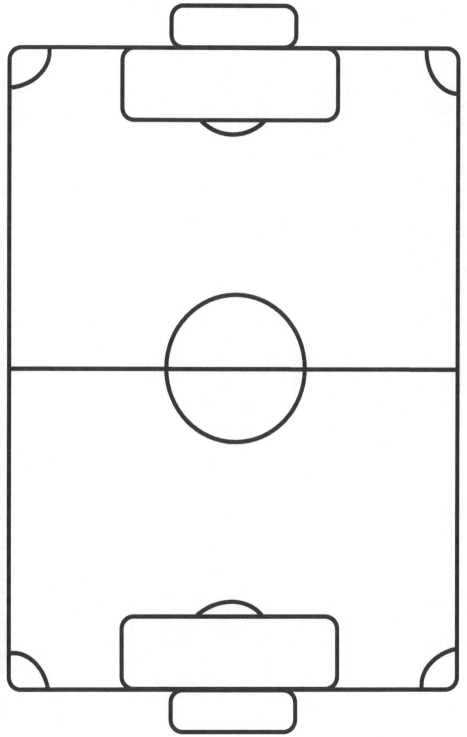

or even some soccer doodles

Tactics and Strategy Ideas

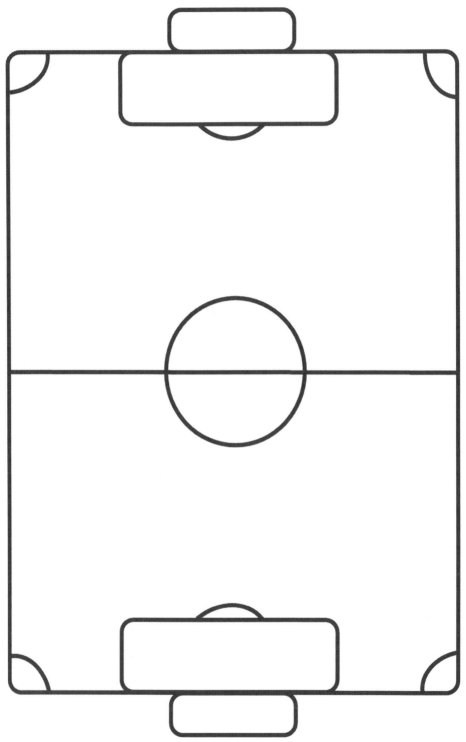

or even some soccer doodles

Tactics and Strategy Ideas

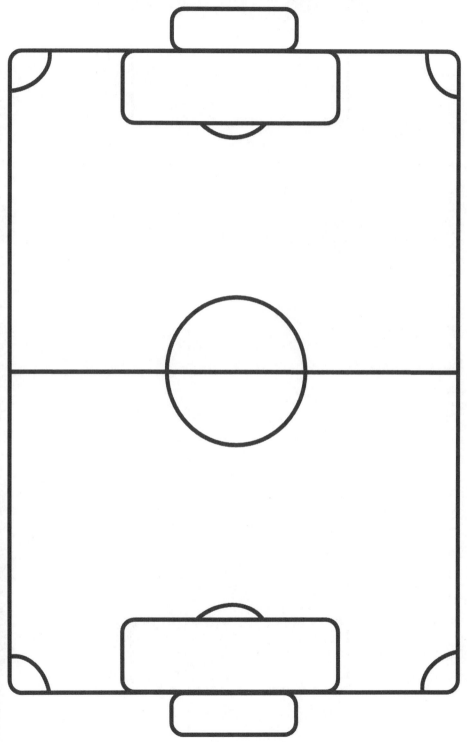

or even some soccer doodles

Tactics and Strategy Ideas

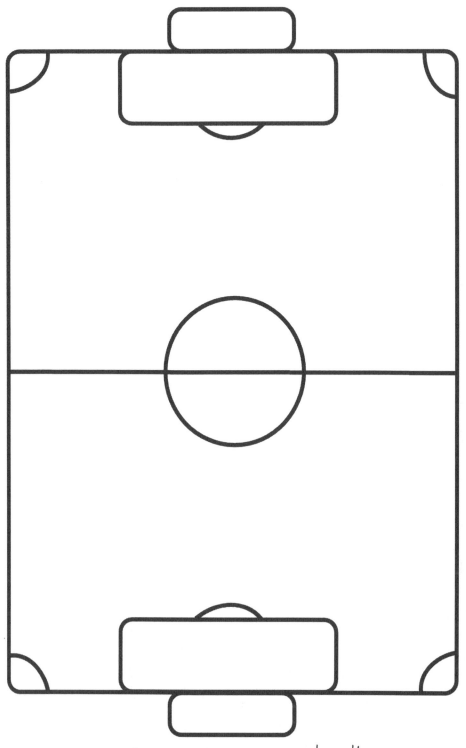

or even some soccer doodles

Tactics and Strategy Ideas

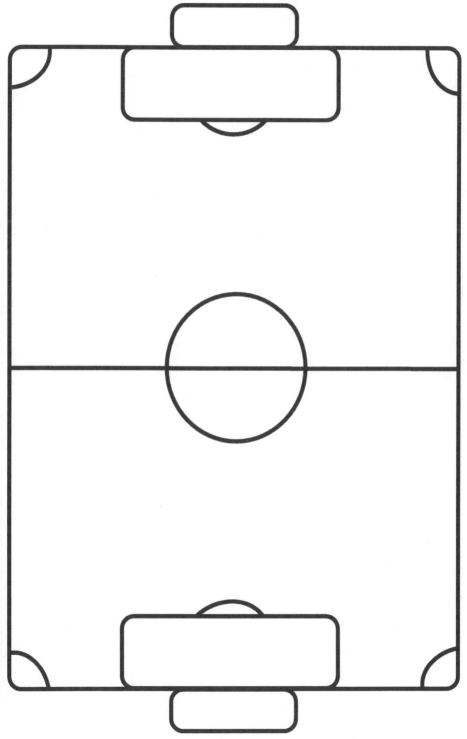

or even some soccer doodles

Tactics and Strategy Ideas

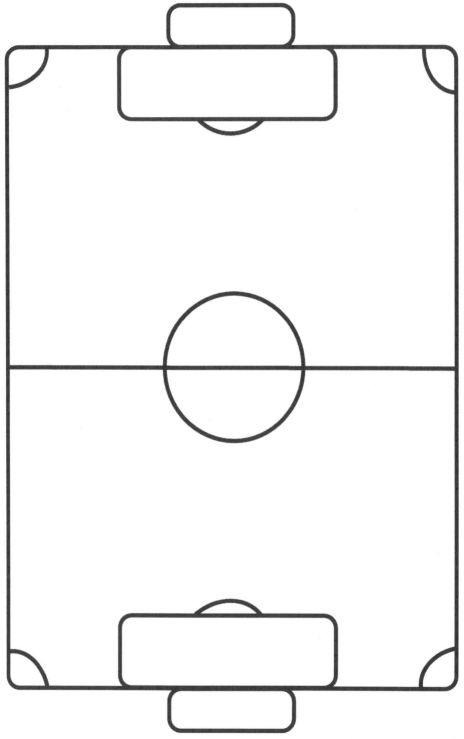

or even some soccer doodles

Made in the USA
Columbia, SC
17 March 2020